FAR-OUT GUIDE TO

JUPITER

Mary Kay Carson

Bailey Books
an imprint of
Enslow Publishers, Inc.
40 Industrial Road
Box 398
Berkeley Heights, NJ 07922
USA
http://www.enslow.com

For Ezra James Schelly, whose heart is as big as Jupiter

Bailey Books, an imprint of Enslow Publishers, Inc.

Copyright © 2011 by Mary Kay Carson

Library of Congress Cataloging-in-Publication Data

Carson, Mary Kay.
    Far-out guide to Jupiter / Mary Kay Carson.
      p. cm. — (Far-out guide to the solar system)
    Includes bibliographical references and index.
    Summary: "Presents information about Jupiter, including fast facts, history,
and technology used to study the planet"—Provided by publisher.
    ISBN 978-0-7660-3184-5 (Library Ed.)
    ISBN 978-1-59845-186-3 (Paperback Ed.)
    1. Jupiter (Planet)—Juvenile literature. 2. Solar system—Juvenile literature. I. Title.
QB661.C376 2011
523.45—dc22
                        2008050036

Printed in China

052010 Leo Paper Group, Heshan City, Guangdong, China

10 9 8 7 6 5 4 3 2 1

To Our Readers: We have done our best to make sure all Internet Addresses in this book were active and appropriate when we went to press. However, the author and the publisher have no control over and assume no liability for the material available on those Internet sites or on other Web sites they may link to. Any comments or suggestions can be sent by e-mail to comments@enslow.com or to the address on the back cover.

Photo Credits: Hubble Space Telescope Comet Team and NASA, p. 10; Michael Carroll and NASA, pp. 1, 23; NASA, pp. 9, 11; NASA/JPL, pp. 3, 4-5, 6 (bottom), 13, 14, 15, 18, 24, 26, 27, 29, 30, 32, 34, 36, 39; NASA/JPL/University of Arizona, p. 6 (top); Reprinted with permission of Carnegie Mellon University, Pittsburgh, Pennsylvania. www.cmu.edu, p. 42; X-ray: NASA/CXC/SwRI/R.Gladstone et al.; Optical: NASA/ESA/Hubble Heritage (AURA/STScI), p. 41.

Cover Photo: Michael Carroll and NASA

Cover image: Illustration of the Galileo *spacecraft at Jupiter's moon Amalthea in 2002*

CONTENTS

Jupiter

JUPITER is the largest planet in our solar system, and the fifth from the Sun. (Note that the planets' distances are not shown to scale.)

INTRODUCTION

On Jupiter, there is a storm called the Great Red Spot. This huge storm has been raging for at least 300 years! How do we know this? Astronomers have been watching the storm with telescopes for centuries. More recently, robotic space-craft have sent back a close-up view of the swirling storm. You will learn lots more far-out facts about Jupiter in this book. Just keep reading!

Jupiter is gigantic. It is bigger than any other planet in our solar system. Imagine gathering up the seven other planets—twice. Now squash all 14 together. This planetary ball is big, but amazingly, Jupiter is still bigger! You could stuff more than 1,300 Earths inside Jupiter. You cannot stuff that many peas into a sandwich bag. Jupiter is enormous!

IO, the moon of Jupiter in this photograph, is about the size of Earth's moon. But it looks tiny next to gigantic Jupiter!

WHAT DOES BIGGEST MEAN?

There are three different ways to compare planet sizes. Mass is how much matter is in something. Mass is measured in kilograms. Volume is how much space something fills. A planet's volume is often compared to Earth's volume. As with any sphere, the distance through a planet's center is its diameter. Diameter is measured in miles or kilometers. Jupiter is the biggest planet in all three ways! Check out Jupiter's mass, volume, and diameter on page 18.

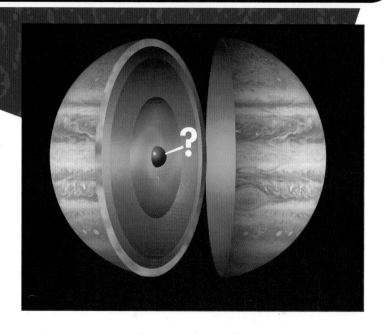

JUPITER'S layers are mostly liquids and gases. Space scientists think Jupiter's core is solid, but they are not sure what kind of solid. It may be ice, rock, or metal.

Even though Jupiter is the biggest planet in the solar system, it is hard to study. No spacecraft could ever land there, because there is no land! Jupiter is a gas giant planet. Like Saturn, Uranus, and Neptune, it is a world made mostly of gases. Most of its gases are under so much pressure that they have been squashed into liquids.

Space probes from Earth have visited Jupiter. These robotic explorers have taught us a lot about the King of Planets. They have discovered rings and studied centuries-old storms. Spacecraft have checked out Jupiter's moons, too. Unlike Jupiter, these smaller worlds have land—and likely even have oceans under their surfaces. Now scientists want to find out if anything swims in them.

Being gigantic gives Jupiter a lot of pull in its neighborhood. Gravitational pull, that is! The more massive an object, the more gravity it has. Jupiter tugs on everything near it, including over sixty moons. Jupiter's gravity also pulls in a lot of passing asteroids and comets. That has kept the rest of our solar system a bit safer. Being slammed by an asteroid or comet can be hard on a planet!

CHAPTER I

A GIANT WITH STRIPES

It was 1994. After traveling for nearly five years, the *Galileo* space probe was just arriving at Jupiter. A space shuttle had launched it in 1989, and everything went fine at first. Then *Galileo* tried to open its big antenna. It got stuck. Engineers on Earth worked hard to fix the problem. They sent lots of new instructions to *Galileo*. Its other antenna eventually had to take over. Luckily the space probe was ready and able to catch a great view of Jupiter gobbling up a comet. The comet's name was Shoemaker-Levy 9. It had flown too close to Jupiter. The planet's gravity grabbed the comet, pulled it in, and ripped it apart. Soon comet chunks crashed into Jupiter. *Galileo* was able to take photos of the comet's crash with Jupiter.

THIS illustration shows the *Galileo* spacecraft at Jupiter. The probe was about the size of a bus.

ROBOTIC EXPLORERS

Space probes are robotic explorers. They are uncrewed spacecraft, meaning they have no astronauts on board. Space probes come in different shapes, sizes, and sorts. Three kinds of space probes have visited Jupiter—flyby, orbiter, and atmospheric probes. Flyby probes collect information and take photographs of a planet or moon as they fly by it. An orbiter space probe goes into orbit around a planet or moon, circling it many times. An atmospheric probe travels through a planet's or moon's atmosphere, collecting weather information as it descends.

COMET chunks exploded into Jupiter like bombs. Each explosion created giant dark dust clouds, like the ones seen here. Some were twice as wide as Earth!

PROBING THE GIANT

By the time *Galileo* photographed the comet crash, the spacecraft was in good shape. It was ready to explore Jupiter. What was on its to-do list? Launch a probe into Jupiter's atmosphere. It was "white-knuckle time," said Richard Young. Young is a scientist who worked at the National Aeronautics and Space Administration (NASA). He headed the team in charge of *Galileo*'s atmospheric probe. He also helped design and build it. Now it was showtime.

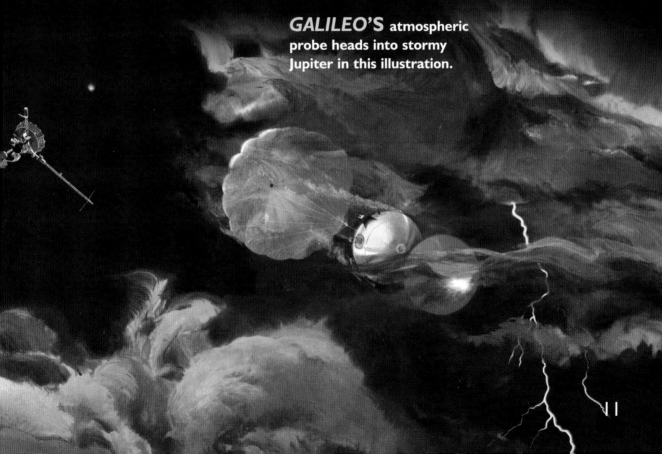

GALILEO'S atmospheric probe heads into stormy Jupiter in this illustration.

Young's job was to make sure the probe worked perfectly. First, it had to hit the atmosphere at the right angle. Then it had to slow down—fast. Otherwise it would not have time to take weather measurements. Jupiter's atmosphere gradually gets thicker toward the planet's center. Eventually, the thick atmosphere would squash the probe. "Imagine Jupiter is a tomato," said Young. "We were only going to pierce the skin of the tomato." Everyone knew it would be a short trip.

Galileo released the atmospheric probe toward the giant planet in July 1995. The small probe traveled toward Jupiter for five months. On December 7, 1995, it finally reached Jupiter's atmosphere. It plunged down toward the planet so fast that its speed would have taken it across the United States in 100 seconds. A parachute opened and slowed the probe down. The probe took measurements in the atmosphere as it dropped. It measured temperature, pressure, chemicals, and clouds. The probe lasted about an hour before Jupiter crushed and melted it. But it successfully sent its gathered data. "There were a lot of surprises," said Young. Jupiter was windier than scientists had thought. Winds roared at 531 kilometers

JUPITER'S Great Red Spot is a giant, ancient storm. It has been raging for at least 300 years. It is about twice as wide as Earth, though its size varies.

(330 miles) per hour. There were fewer watery clouds and less lightning than scientists had expected, too.

CIRCLING STORMS

The probe did an important job. Scientists wanted to learn about Jupiter's weather. This was "one of the major science goals for *Galileo*," explained Young. The *Galileo* spacecraft also studied weather. It began circling, or orbiting, Jupiter. *Galileo* became the first gas giant orbiter. An orbiter spacecraft can find out more than a flyby probe. Making loops around Jupiter gave *Galileo* lots of long looks at the planet.

What did *Galileo* see on Jupiter? Wild weather! Monster storms rage. Fierce winds blow. Lighting flashes, and clouds swirl with ammonia, one of the chemicals in window cleaner.

Some of Jupiter's thunderstorms are a thousand times the size of ours. The Sun's heat fuels storms on Earth, but sunlight cannot create storms on Jupiter. It is too far away. Sunlight is only 4 percent as strong on Jupiter

GALILEO took this false-color image of Jupiter's clouds. The colors have been made brighter to show the different layers. The light blue clouds are high and thin. Red clouds are deep. High, thick clouds are white. Haze is purple.

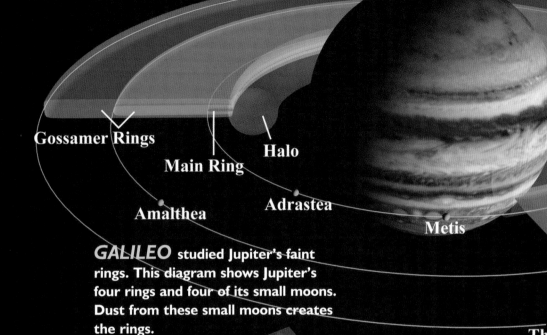

Gossamer Rings

Main Ring

Halo

Amalthea

Adrastea

Metis

GALILEO studied Jupiter's faint rings. This diagram shows Jupiter's four rings and four of its small moons. Dust from these small moons creates the rings.

Thebe

HISTORY-MAKING SPACECRAFT

Galileo racked up a bunch of "space firsts" during its long mission.

- First space probe to orbit, or loop around, a gas giant planet.

- First Jupiter orbiter space probe. (Earlier space probes only flew by Jupiter.)

- First spacecraft to drop an atmospheric probe into a gas giant.

- First flyby of an asteroid. *Galileo* flew by asteroid Gaspra in 1991.

- Discovered first moon around an asteroid. *Galileo* photographed tiny moon Dactyl orbiting asteroid Ida in 1993.

as it is on Earth. So what fuels Jupiter's stormy weather? Galileo scientists think it is heat from deep inside the giant planet.

A HEROIC END

Galileo orbited for eight years. But nothing lasts forever. By 2003, *Galileo* was low on fuel. It had traveled nearly 4.8 billion kilometers (3 billion miles)! That included 34 trips around the giant planet. Scientists made a tough call. They decided to crash *Galileo* into Jupiter. Galileo scientists got together for its final moments. They hugged as Jupiter's pressure and heat crushed and burned up the spacecraft.

Galileo doomed itself when it made an important discovery. It found something amazing on Europa, one of Jupiter's biggest moons. Scientists knew an ocean under Europa's icy surface was a possibility. Information and images from the *Voyager* space probes had hinted at it more than twenty years earlier. But the information *Galileo* collected during eleven trips around Europa provided more evidence. The icy moon likely has an ocean of liquid water. *Galileo*'s discovery of Europa's ocean was the reason scientists decided to burn up the probe. NASA could not risk having *Galileo* sputter off course, which could have happened as its fuel ran out. It might have accidentally crashed on Europa and harmed something there. Who knows what might be in that under-ice ocean? Some sort of life might exist on Europa.

FAR-OUT FACT

HOW BIG IS IT?

Jupiter is big and bright enough to see from Earth without a telescope. This huge planet is not close to Earth. The distance from Jupiter to Earth is five times the distance from the Sun to Earth, but its mega size makes Jupiter one of the brightest objects in our night sky. Only Venus and the Moon are brighter. (Want to spot Jupiter at night? See page 47.) The ancient Romans watched this big bright object in the night sky, too. They named it after the king of their gods, Jupiter.

JUPITER AT A GLANCE

Diameter: 142,984 kilometers (88,846 miles)

Volume: 1,316 Earths

Mass: 318 Earths, or 1,898,700,000,000,000 trillion kilograms

Position: Fifth planet from the Sun

Average Distance from Sun: 778 million kilometers (484 million miles)

Day Length: 9 hours, 56 minutes

Year Length: 4,331 Earth days (almost 12 Earth years)

Color: Orange with stripes

Atmosphere: 86% hydrogen; 14% helium

Surface: None

Temperature: −148° Celsius (−234° Fahrenheit)

Moons: 62

Rings: 4

Namesake: King of the Roman gods

Symbol:

Planet Fast Facts

★ Jupiter is the largest planet in our solar system. It has the most mass, the largest volume, and the greatest diameter of all the planets in our solar system.

★ More than 1,300 Earths could fit inside Jupiter.

★ It takes nearly a dozen Earth years for Jupiter to travel around the Sun once.

★ Sunlight is only 4 percent as strong on Jupiter as it is on Earth.

★ Jupiter is five times as far from the Sun as Earth is.

★ All planets spin, or rotate, like a top. The time it takes to make one spin, or rotation, is called a day. Jupiter spins really fast. It rotates more than twice during an Earth day.

★ Jupiter has a magnetic field nearly 20,000 times as powerful as Earth's. The region of space it affects, its magnetosphere, extends hundreds of millions of kilometers away from Jupiter.

★ Radio waves from Jupiter's magnetic field reach all the way to Earth.

★ Jupiter has the brightest auroras in the solar system.

★ What looks like a faint ring around Jupiter is actually four narrow rings.

★ Jupiter and its many moons are so big that together they are often called the Jovian system. (*Jovian* is the adjective for *Jupiter*.) The solar system has the Sun at its center. The Jovian system has Jupiter.

★ Jupiter is a gas giant planet. It is a spinning ball of gas and liquid.

★ There is no land on Jupiter.

★ Scientists think that Jupiter might have a solid core.

★ Jupiter's colored stripes are bands of icy clouds made of different kinds of chemicals. Winds push these cloud belts at different speeds.

★ Winds can blow up to 644 kilometers (400 miles) per hour on Jupiter. The planet's speedy spin and rising internal heat create its strong winds.

★ Jupiter's Great Red Spot is a giant storm. It has been going for at least 300 years.

★ Jupiter is easily seen in the night sky without a telescope. Only the Moon and Venus are brighter.

★ Thousands of years ago, many ancient peoples tracked Jupiter's movements across the night sky, including the Egyptians, Greeks, Babylonians, Chinese, and Polynesians.

Moons Fast Facts

★ Sixteen of Jupiter's 62 moons are 10 kilometers (6 miles) or larger in diameter. They are (closest to Jupiter first): Metis, Adrastea, Amalthea, Thebe, Io, Europa, Ganymede, Callisto, Leda, Himalia, Lysithea, Elara, Ananke, Carme, Pasiphae, and Sinope.

★ Many of Jupiter's small outer moons were probably asteroids caught by the planet's gravity. The larger moons probably formed alongside Jupiter when the planet itself took shape.

★ Italian astronomer Galileo Galilei discovered Jupiter's four largest moons in 1610. Callisto, Europa, Ganymede, and Io are now known as the Galilean moons.

★ Ganymede is the largest moon in our solar system. It is larger than the planet Mercury.

★

* ★ Europa may have an ocean under its icy surface.
* ★ Io has more active volcanoes than any other known moon.
* ★ Callisto is covered in more craters than any other known moon or planet.
* ★ Astronomers on Earth discovered 22 of Jupiter's moons in 2003.

Mission Fast Facts

* ★ No astronauts, only robotic space probes, have traveled to Jupiter.
* ★ Spaceships will never land on Jupiter. There is no land.
* ★ *Pioneer 10* was the first spacecraft to visit Jupiter, the first to travel past Mars, and the first to fly through the asteroid belt.
* ★ *Voyager 1* discovered Jupiter's rings.
* ★ *Galileo* was the first spacecraft to orbit Jupiter.
* ★ *Galileo* carried the first atmospheric probe to Jupiter.
* ★ Some spacecraft visit Jupiter on their way elsewhere. They can get a gravity boost from the planet, which flings them on their way.

Jupiter Timeline

of Exploration and Discovery

(Years given for missions are when spacecraft explored Jupiter. These explorations happened years after launch.)

PREHISTORY Ancient peoples watch this bright, shining object in the night sky.

1610 Galileo Galilei discovers the moons Callisto, Europa, Ganymede, and Io using his newly improved telescope.

1655 Giovanni Cassini discovers Jupiter's Great Red Spot.

1892 Edward Barnard discovers the moon Amalthea.

1973 *Pioneer 10* is the first spacecraft to visit Jupiter. The flyby probe passes within 130,000 kilometers (81,000 miles) of Jupiter's clouds.

1974 *Pioneer 11* flies by Jupiter. The flyby probe comes within 43,000 kilometers (26,725 miles) of the planet's clouds. The spacecraft studies Jupiter's magnetic field and atmosphere. It takes pictures of Jupiter and some of its moons.

1979 *Voyager 1* and *Voyager 2* pass by Jupiter and its moons. The two flyby probes take more than 33,000 pictures. They discover Jupiter's rings and moons Thebe, Metis, and Adrastea.

1992 *Ulysses* flies by Jupiter on its way to study the Sun.

1994 Space probe *Galileo*, the *Hubble Space Telescope*, and Earth-based telescopes watch comet Shoemaker-Levy 9 crash into Jupiter.

★

1995 *Galileo*'s atmospheric probe plunges toward Jupiter. It is the first atmospheric probe to a gas giant planet. It sends back weather information for nearly an hour.

1995–2003 *Galileo* orbits Jupiter, studying the planet and its moons for eight years. It finds evidence of an ocean under Europa's icy surface and watches volcanoes erupt on Io.

2000 *Cassini* spacecraft takes pictures of Jupiter on its way to orbit Saturn.

2003 Astronomers on Earth discover 22 new moons circling Jupiter using giant telescopes in Hawaii.

2007 Pluto-bound space probe *New Horizons* flies by Jupiter. It snaps pictures of new storms and studies Jupiter's rings.

2016 *Jupiter Polar Orbiter* (*Juno*) spacecraft to arrive at Jupiter after a scheduled 2011 launch to study its magnetosphere and look for a solid core.

THIS illustration shows *Galileo* at Jupiter's moon Amalthea in 2002.

23

JUPITER'S four biggest moons are (top to bottom): Io, Europa, Ganymede, and Callisto. (Note that these moons are not shown in actual orbit.)

CHAPTER 2

WORLDS OF FIRE AND ICE

Gigantic Jupiter has more than 60 moons. The largest moons are Io, Europa, Ganymede, and Callisto. Io and Europa are about the size of our Moon. Ganymede and Callisto are closer to Mercury's size. These four moons are extra interesting. Each of the four is a unique world. All are worlds worth exploring.

VOLCANIC MOON

"Io, of course, is my favorite," said Rosaly Lopes. It is easy to understand why. Lopes is a volcano scientist. "We have found more than one hundred volcanoes on Io," she said. Lopes worked on *Galileo*'s science team studying Io's volcanoes. One of those volcanoes is called Loki. It is the biggest volcano in the solar system. Loki has more power than all of Earth's volcanoes put together. Io's lava is also hotter

FAR-OUT FACT

GALILEO'S MOONS

Jupiter's four largest moons—Io, Europa, Ganymede, and Callisto—are called the Galilean moons because they were discovered by Galileo Galilei. The Italian scientist first saw the moons in 1610. He spotted them with his newly improved telescope. Want to remember the order of Galileo's largest moons, from closest to farthest from Jupiter? Think: I Eat Graham Crackers. The first letters match those of the four moons: Io, Europa, Ganymede, Callisto. What else was named after Galileo? The *Galileo* spacecraft!

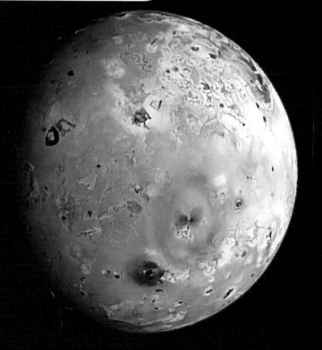

IO is covered in volcanoes. Its largest volcano, Loki, is the black horseshoe shape on the left. The giant red ring was created by volcano Pele.

than any on Earth today. "Billions of years ago, Earth had lava that hot," said Lopes. Io's volcanoes let us peek in on Earth's past.

Io is a cold world. The sun barely shines there. Temperatures on the surface are about −145 degrees Celsius (−230 degrees Fahrenheit)! How can it have such hot volcanoes? A kind of tug-of-war causes Io's volcanoes. Jupiter's gravity pulls hard on Io. The other big moons pull on Io, too. And all the pulls are in different directions. This pushing and pulling squeezes Io's insides.

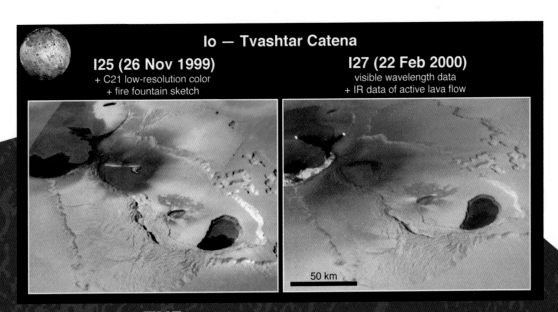

Io — Tvashtar Catena

I25 (26 Nov 1999)
+ C21 low-resolution color
+ fire fountain sketch

I27 (22 Feb 2000)
visible wavelength data
+ IR data of active lava flow

50 km

THE *Galileo* spacecraft caught this volcano at work on Io. The left picture was taken a few months before the right picture. Can you see the new lava on the right?

FAR-OUT FACT

MORE MOONS, PLEASE

Jupiter has many moons: at least 62—and counting! We have known about some of Jupiter's moons for centuries. Spacecraft have discovered others. *Voyager 1* found three new moons in 1979. The biggest boost to Jupiter's moon family came in 2003. That year astronomers on Earth discovered 22 new moons! How? They used a giant telescope on top of a Hawaiian mountain. Many of these new moons are small. Some were probably once asteroids.

The squeezing heats up Io's inner rocks. If melted rock breaks through the moon's surface, it creates a volcano.

Volcanoes are not the only thing Rosaly Lopes likes. She has been a fan of space since childhood. Lopes grew up in Brazil, and watched the moon landings when she was a kid. That made her want to be an astronaut, but "being from Brazil and a girl, my chances were not too great," she said. Studying astronomy was odd enough.

"Everybody thought I was crazy," said Lopes. Now she explores space through science. Lopes loves discovering new things, she says, like "new volcanoes on Io! We found many more volcanoes on Io than we expected." The scientist and her team discovered 71 new volcanoes on Io. She named two of them Tupan and Monan. They are named after native Brazilian gods of thunder and fire.

SCIENTIST Rosaly Lopes studies volcanoes on other planets and their moons, but she likes Earth volcanoes, too. She visits the ones on Earth whenever she can.

PLANETLIKE MOON

Galileo found surprises on each of Jupiter's four big moons. And no moon is bigger than Ganymede—at least not in our solar system. Ganymede is big enough to be a planet. It is larger than Mercury! But Ganymede is a moon because it orbits another planet. A planet must orbit the Sun. Ganymede does have some planet characteristics, including mountains and valleys and a very thin

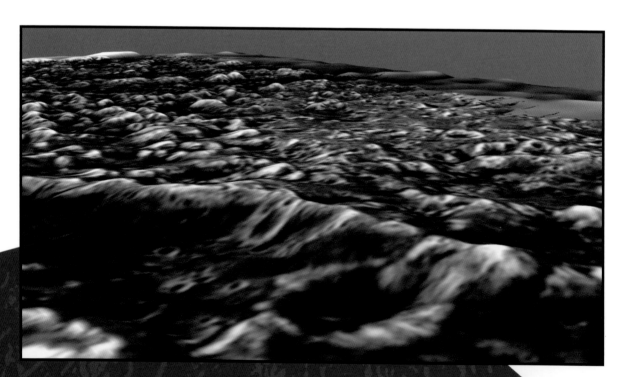

THIS three-dimensional picture of Ganymede shows its hilly surface.

FAR-OUT FACT

MAGNET-O-WHAT?

Earth's got one. Jupiter's is really big. And even Ganymede's got one. But what is a magnetosphere? It is the region of space affected by a world's magnetic field. This field acts upon anything attracted or repelled by magnetism—like a paper clip near a household magnet. A planet's magnetic field gives it north and south magnetic poles. A magnetic field is what makes a compass needle move. Jupiter is like an upside down magnet compared to Earth. On Jupiter, an Earth compass would read south when pointing north!

atmosphere. None of Jupiter's moons have breathable air, but a tiny bit of oxygen surrounds Ganymede.

One *Galileo* discovery about Ganymede shocked scientists. This massive moon has a magnetosphere. It is "something no one thought a moon would have," said Rosaly Lopes. No other moon does. How does Ganymede make its own magnetic field? Probably the same way

Earth makes one. Melted metal sloshes around inside the moon, creating a current of electric charges that acts like a giant magnet. But Ganymede's magnetosphere is hard to notice, because Jupiter's magnetic field is much bigger! Jupiter's magnetosphere is the largest object in the solar system. It is even bigger than the Sun!

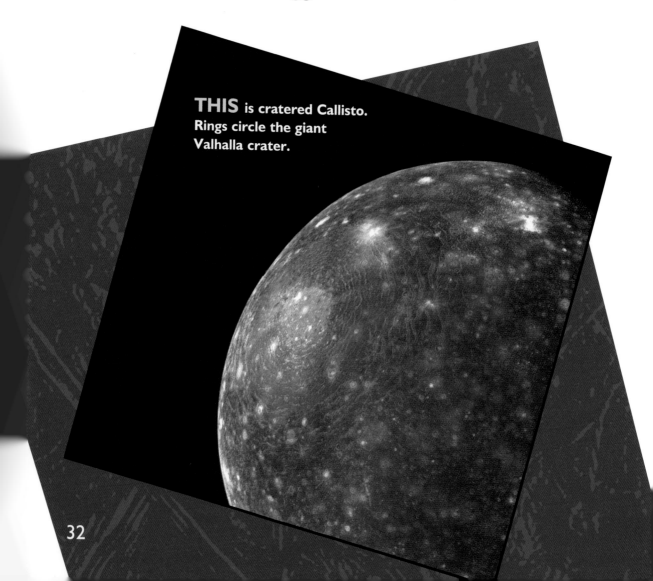

THIS is cratered Callisto. Rings circle the giant Valhalla crater.

CRATERED MOON

Callisto is the Galilean moon farthest from Jupiter. Craters cover nearly all of Callisto. Hundreds of asteroids and comets have left their mark on its surface. Callisto has more craters than any other known moon or planet. One gigantic crater is called Valhalla. It is as big as Australia! At least 25 rings of wrinkled moon surface circle the crater. Why so many? Callisto has a thin icy surface that can be cracked easily. The wrinkles are like the rings left when a ball slams into a frozen puddle.

Like our Moon, Callisto is a "dead world" whose ancient surface has not changed in a long time. No surface-erasing lava flows exist, like on Io. And no mountains have formed, like on Ganymede. But Callisto could be a bit like Europa. Beneath its icy surface might be water.

LIVING OCEAN OR LIFELESS MOON?

It was *Galileo*'s biggest discovery. The one that doomed it. "Europa has most likely an ocean of liquid water," said Lopes. The ocean is under an icy surface. Why is the deep water not frozen? There is heat inside Europa—the same

A zoomed-in look at Europa shows its streaked, icy surface.

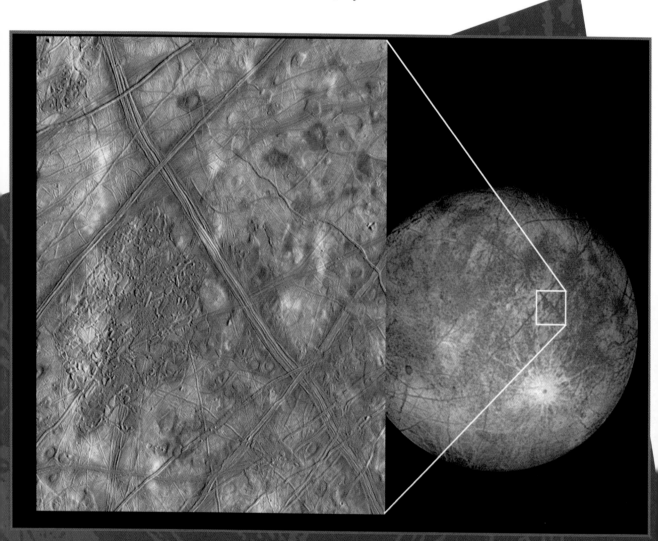

kind of heat that powers Io's volcanoes. Heat and water "are two of the ingredients you need for life," explained Lopes. With that possiblity for life, no one could let *Galileo* crash into Europa. Engineers steered the spacecraft into Jupiter instead. *Galileo* put Europa on scientists' lists of places to look for alien life.

FAR-OUT FACT

EUROPA ON EARTH?

Europa is not Earth. But there are places on our planet that are a bit like this Jovian moon. One place is on an arctic island in northern Canada. It is called Borup Fiord Pass. There, mineral springs stain the permanent ice. (Sound familiar?) Scientists are looking for mineral-munching microbes in the ice. Another icy place is Lake Vostok, Antarctica. This lake is always frozen under miles of Antarctic ice. Scientists found microbes living in the water more than 3.2 kilometers (2 miles) deep.

WHAT is under Europa's ice? This illustration shows one idea. Underwater volcanoes might keep the ocean water from freezing.

Another thing that interests scientists is that Europa's icy surface changes. It is not cratered and dead. Europa is crisscrossed with cracks and colored streaks. Scientists think these streaks could be minerals spewed up by volcanoes under the ice. Undersea volcanoes make chemical energy. We know creatures use this kind of energy to live in Earth's deep, dark oceans. Maybe they do on Europa, too. Looking under Europa's thick icy surface is the only way to find out.

CHAPTER 3

WHAT'S NEXT FOR JUPITER?

Do you want to understand how our solar system started and where the planets came from? Then you need to understand Jupiter. Most of the solar system's planetary mass is Jupiter. How did Jupiter form—and when? What is inside Jupiter? Does Jupiter have a metal core? What is under those thick, colorful clouds?

JUNO TO JUPITER

Answering these questions is *Juno*'s job. *Juno* is the short name for the *Jupiter Polar Orbiter*. It is the next mission to Jupiter, set to launch in 2011. It will ride on a rocket to space. Then *Juno* will unfold its three solar panels. It will fly to Jupiter powered by the Sun! Its journey to the giant planet will take five years.

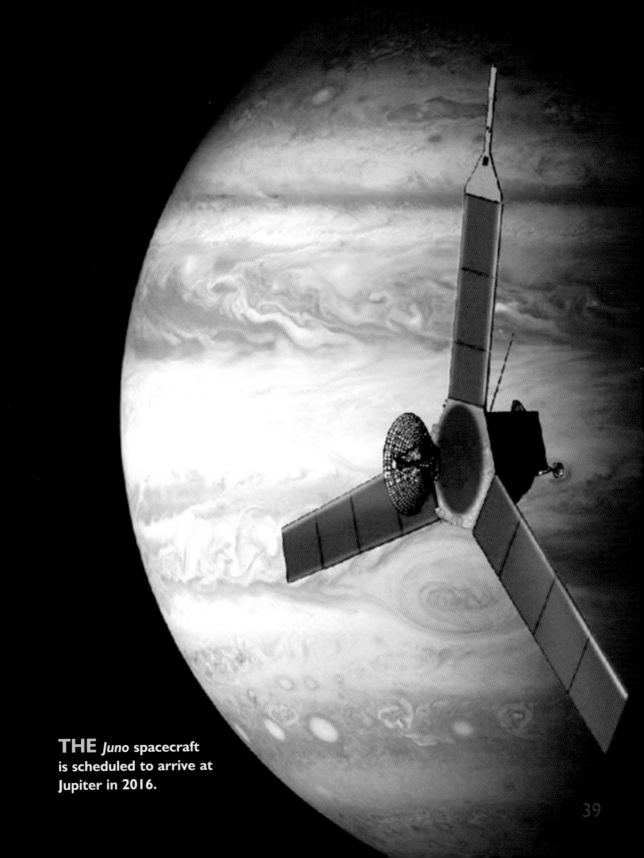

THE *Juno* spacecraft
is scheduled to arrive at
Jupiter in 2016.

PRODUCTIVE PIT STOP

In late 2007, the *New Horizons* space probe flew by Jupiter on its way to Pluto. While grabbing a gravity boost, the small spacecraft made some fantastic observations of giant Jupiter. It found wild weather, like lightning, at the planet's poles, and clouds of ammonia bubbling up from the lower atmosphere. *New Horizons* also snapped the first close-up photos of a storm the size of Mars, called the Little Red Spot, and the best yet images of Jupiter's faint rings.

Once at Jupiter, *Juno* will go into orbit. It is not called a "polar orbiter" for nothing! *Juno* will circle the planet's poles in a long, oval loop. This will keep it out of the way of Jupiter's magnetosphere. Jupiter's magnetic field is super powerful. Flying through it would fry the spacecraft's electronics. You would not leave an MP3 player next to a stack of magnets for the same reason.

Juno will collect information in orbit. One of *Juno's* instruments will map Jupiter's insides. Will it find a metal core? Maybe. Something has to be making that massive magnetosphere! *Juno* will also study a showy effect of Jupiter's magnetic field. Jupiter has huge auroras, or glowing bands of light near its poles. Did you know that

AN X-ray telescope called *Chandra* took these pictures of Jupiter in 2007. Jupiter's auroras glow brighter than any others in the solar system.

SCIENTISTS are working on robot submarines to explore Europa. This one is called **DEPTHX**. It can dive deep and explore in the dark—without real-time instructions.

WHAT ABOUT EUROPA?

No one is forgetting about Europa. Space scientists are coming up with plans to send a spacecraft there—someday. When it might launch has not been decided. Looking for life on Europa is a tough mission. The spacecraft will need to drill through ice many kilometers thick. Then a robot submarine can slip under the ice. The robot will have to search for alien life on its own. Europa is too far away to send and receive instant radio instructions from Earth. *Galileo*'s radio signals from Jupiter took fifty minutes to reach Earth.

Earth has auroras, too? We call our auroras the Northern Lights and the Southern Lights. But Jupiter has the brightest auroras in our solar system. Jupiter's fast-spinning magnetosphere makes its auroras very bright. Charged particles hitting Jupiter flash with light. Some of those particles come from the Sun. (Earth's auroras are caused this way.) Other particles come from Io's volcanoes.

Other instruments on *Juno* will measure heat and water. Jupiter has lots of frozen water. Because it is so big, Jupiter has most of the solar system's water. Knowing exactly how much water is important. It will give scientists clues about Jupiter's beginnings. It will also tell us something about how Earth got its water. Jupiter's history is Earth's history, too. Scientists believe that both formed out of the same cloud of dust and gas from which all the planets formed. They all once swirled together around the Sun. Most of that cloud ended up as Jupiter, making it the gigantic planet it is today.

Words to Know

antenna—**A rod or wire that sends and/or receives radio waves.**

asteroid—**A large rock, smaller than a planet, that orbits the Sun.**

asteroid belt—**The region of space between Mars and Jupiter where most asteroids are found.**

astronomer—**A scientist who studies moons, stars, planets, and the universe.**

astronomy—**The study of moons, stars, planets, galaxies, and the universe.**

atmosphere—**The gases that are held by gravity around a planet, moon, or other object in space.**

atmospheric probe—**A space probe that studies the atmosphere of a planet or moon while passing though it.**

aurora—**Lights near a planet's poles caused by charged particles hitting its atmosphere.**

charged particles—**Tiny bits of matter with electrical charges, including electrons, protons, and ions.**

comet—**A large chunk of frozen gases, ice, and dust that orbits the Sun.**

core—**The center, usually solid, of a planet or moon.**

craters—**Bowl-shaped holes made by impact explosions on the surface of a planet or moon, often from comet or asteroid crashes.**

diameter—**A straight line through the center of a sphere.**

engineer—**Someone who designs machines.**

flyby probe—**A space probe that flies by a planet or moon.**

gas giant—**A planet made of mostly gas and liquid with no land, such as Jupiter, Saturn, Uranus, and Neptune.**

gravitational pull—**An attractive force on one object from another.**

gravity—**The force of attraction between two or more bodies that have mass.**

ion—**An electrically charged particle.**

magnetic field—**The area of magnetic influence around a magnet, electric current, or planet.**

magnetosphere—**The region of space affected by the magnetic field of a planet or moon.**

mass—**The amount of matter in something.**

microbe—**A living thing too small to be seen without a microscope.**

orbit—**The path followed by a planet, moon, or other object around another object in space; to move around an object in space.**

orbiter—**A space probe that orbits a planet, moon, or other object in space.**

pole—**One of two points on a sphere farthest from the equator; or either end of a magnet.**

pressure (atmospheric)—**The force on a surface from the weight of the air pushing down on it.**

space probe—**A robotic spacecraft launched into space to collect information.**

volume—**The amount of space something fills.**

Find Out More and Get Updates

Books

Aguilar, David A. *11 Planets: A New View of the Solar System.* Washington, D.C.: National Geographic Children's Books, 2008.

Birch, Robin. *Jupiter.* New York: Chelsea House Publishers, 2008.

Carson, Mary Kay. *Exploring the Solar System: A History with 22 Activities.* Chicago: Chicago Review Press, 2008.

Fraknoi, Andrew. *Disney's Wonderful World of Space.* New York: Disney Publishing, 2007.

Graham, Ian. *Space Vehicles.* Chicago: Raintree, 2006.

Jefferis, David. *Mighty Megaplanets: Jupiter and Saturn.* New York: Crabtree Publishing Co., 2009.

Solar System Web Sites

You will find lots more information on Jupiter—and fun space stuff—on these Web sites.

NASA. "Solar System Exploration." 2008.
  <http://solarsystem.nasa.gov/kids/>

Windows to the Universe. "Jupiter." 2004.
  <http://www.windows.ucar.edu/tour/link=/jupiter/jupiter.html>

Jupiter Missions Web Sites

Read about past missions, check out amazing pictures, and get updates on the next missions to Jupiter and its moons.

"Juno: NASA's New Frontiers Mission to Jupiter." 2008.
  <http://juno.wisc.edu/>

NASA/JPL. "Galileo Project Home." 2003.
  <http://www2.jpl.nasa.gov/galileo/>

Planet-watching Web Sites

Here are some Web sites to help you find Jupiter and other planets in the night sky.

Astronomy For Kids. "Observe Jupiter's Moons." 2009.
  <http://www.kidsastronomy.com/astroskymap/jup_moons.htm>

StarDate Online. "Planet Viewing." 2009.
  <http://stardate.org/nightsky/planets/>

Index